Lives

BUTTERFLIES

Sally Morgan

QED Publishing

Written by Sally Morgan
Designed by Q2A Solutions
Editor Tom Jackson

Publisher Steve Evans
Creative Director Louise Morley
Editorial Manager Jean Coppendale

Printed and bound in China

Picture Credits

Words in **bold** are
explained in the
Glossary on page 31.

Contents

Butterflies

With their large, colourful wings, butterflies are among the most beautiful of all **insects**. They are often seen fluttering around flowers.

Butterfly bodies

All insects, including butterflies, have three body parts: a head, a middle part called a **thorax** and at the end a part called an **abdomen**. Their eyes and **antennae** (feelers) are attached to the head. Insects also have three pairs of legs and, usually, two pairs of wings which are joined onto the thorax.

A butterfly's wings ca be different shapes.

Metamorphosis

Young butterflies do not look anything like the adults. They hatch from eggs as worm-like **caterpillars**.

A caterpillar grows and then becomes a **pupa**. During this stage, the caterpillar's body changes into an adult butterfly. This change in shape is called **metamorphosis**.

This is the caterpillar of the postman butterfly. The spines along its body help to protect it from **predators**.

Vital statistics

The world's largest butterfly is the Queen Alexandra's birdwing butterfly, which is found only in New Guinea. Females have a wingspan of 28cm. The smallest butterfly in the world is the pygmy blue, with a wingspan of just over 1cm.

Butterfly types

There are about 17 500 different species or types of butterfly in the world. These include the whites, blues and skippers. Swallowtails are among the largest butterflies and have bright wings with colourful spots or bands.

The brush-footed butterflies are named after the brush-like hairs on their forelegs. This large group includes the tortoiseshell and monarch butterflies. The upper surfaces of their wings are brightly coloured, but the undersides are dull. This means that when their wings are folded they are hard to see.

Swallowtails get their name from the 'tails' on their back wings.

Blue morphos have large, shiny blue wings. They are found in the rainforests of Central and South America.

Butterfly or moth?

Butterflies and moths are very similar. However, butterflies have antennae that end in a knob, whereas moth antennae are either slim or feathery. Butterflies fly during the day and when they land, most raise their wings above their body. Moths fly at night and keep their wings flat when resting.

Where do you find butterflies?

Butterflies are found around the world, from the warm regions near the **Equator**, to the colder areas near the Arctic in the north and the southernmost tip of South America. They are not found in the very coldest parts of the world, such as Antarctica.

Butterflies, such as this peacock, are often found in flower-filled meadows.

Butterfly habitats

Butterflies live in almost every habitat where there are plenty of flowers. They are found in meadows, gardens and forests. A few butterflies even live high on mountain slopes and cliff tops. Most, however, live in rainforests. These are shady places, so butterflies are most often spotted flying in sunny clearings.

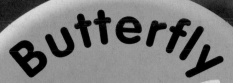

Butterfly fact

The speckled wood butterfly likes to sun itself in sunny spots in woodlands. If another butterfly comes too close, it chases the intruder away.

The black-veined white butterfly is found in woodlands, hedgerows, farmland and in orchards.

9

Butterfly eggs

After a male and female butterfly have **mated**, the female lays her eggs. However, she does not lay them just anywhere. The eggs have to be laid on a plant that the caterpillars can eat. If it is the wrong plant, the caterpillars will starve. Once laid, most eggs hatch after about eight days.

Female butterflies, such as this blue morpho, choose the spot to lay their eggs very carefully.

The tiny caterpillars push their way out of the shell, head first.

Different eggs

All butterfly eggs are small but they vary in colour and shape. The eggs may be laid on the top of a leaf or on its underside. Skippers lay one egg at a time, while the red admiral lays clusters of eggs. Most butterflies will lay several thousand eggs over a few days.

Butterfly fact

Only one in every 100 eggs survives and hatches; the rest are eaten or are killed by diseases.

Caterpillars

A caterpillar looks very different from an adult butterfly. It has a long body made up of many parts, or segments, and no wings.

Body parts

Caterpillars have six very simple eyes, which cannot see detailed images but can pick up movements. They have two short antennae and strong jaws to munch through leaves. Caterpillars walk on six pointed legs and eight stumpy **prolegs**. Prolegs are not proper legs as they end in suckers. Caterpillars have a clasper at the tip of the abdomen which holds onto leaves and stems.

Like all caterpillars, this swallowtail has a body made up of many segments .

Many butterflies lay their eggs in clusters. The young caterpillars stay together for the first week or so after hatching.

Eating all day

Caterpillars do nothing but eat and grow. Like all insects, they have a tough outer covering that does not stretch. As the caterpillar grows, the covering gets too small and must be shed, or **moulted**. This happens about five times.

Butterfly

As it grows, a monarch caterpillar increases its length by about 20 times, and its weight goes up by many thousands of times.

fact

Pupa

When the caterpillar reaches full size, it stops feeding. It moults for the last time and becomes a pupa. Some caterpillars spin a protective cocoon of silk threads around themselves before becoming a pupa.

The shape of the adult blue morpho butterfly can be seen through the wall of this pupa.

Some butterflies spend the winter as a pupa. The caterpillars become pupae in autumn and emerge as adult butterflies in spring.

It takes several hours for the new butterfly's wings to become stiff enough for flying.

Changes

A pupa does not move but, inside, the caterpillar's body is being broken down and reorganized into the shape of an adult butterfly. This may take a few days or several months.

Once the change is complete, the skin of the pupa splits, and an adult butterfly pushes out. Its wings are crumpled up, so the butterfly must pump blood into them so they expand and dry out. Then the new butterfly is ready to fly away.

Butterfly senses

Adult butterflies have two **compound eyes**. Both of these eyes are made up of hundreds of tiny parts that work together. Butterflies can see small movements and they can see colours, including some colours that are invisible to us. This means that many flowers will look very different to a butterfly. For example, they may see dark lines on a petal which we cannot see. The lines lead to where the sugary **nectar** is stored.

Antennae help butterflies to smell and to balance.

This green birdwing butterfly tastes a plant using taste buds on its feet.

Smelling and tasting

Butterflies have a pair of long antennae that they use to pick up smells. They can also taste things using taste buds on their feet! This helps females find the right plant to lay their eggs.

Butterfly

Butterflies flock to 'butterfly bushes', or buddleja, in late summer because the flowers are rich in nectar.

fact

Butterfly flight

A butterfly has two pairs of wings that are hooked together, so the four wings work as if there were just two.

When they **migrate**, monarch butterflies fly in large groups.

Butterfly

A monarch butterfly may fly more than 130 kilometres in a single day.

fact

Long-distance flying

Most butterflies do not usually fly very far, but some make very long journeys. In the summer, many butterflies fly across the English Channel from Europe to Britain. The monarch butterfly flies thousands of kilometres from its summer breeding grounds in the United States to spend the winter in Mexico where it is much warmer.

The scales on the surface of a butterfly's wing look a bit like tiles on a roof.

Scales

A butterfly's wing is covered in tiny scales arranged in rows. The scales have ridges on them that reflect light. The way they reflect light gives the wing its colour. Without the scales, the wing would be transparent, or see-through.

Butterfly food

Adult butterflies do not eat, they only drink. They stay alive by sipping nectar from flowers. Nectar is full of sugar and provides the butterfly with the energy it needs to fly. Butterflies also sip the sugary juice that dribbles from ripe fruits.

A butterfly sucks up nectar using a long feeding tube from its mouth called a **proboscis**. This tube reaches right into the middle of the flower where the nectar is. Butterflies coil up their proboscis under their head when not feeding.

Butterflies prefer to feed on bright flowers that have wide, flat tops.

Like all caterpillars, monarch caterpillars have strong jaws with sharp edges.

Chewers

Caterpillars feed in a very different way from the adults. They have jaws that slice through and chop up tough leaves.

Butterfly fact

Some butterflies drink sap that oozes out of the bark of trees.

Who eats butterflies?

Butterflies are eaten by many animals. Their large, colourful wings make them easy to spot when they fly from flower to flower. Often they are caught by birds. Sometimes they fly into spider webs and get trapped by the sticky threads.

Butterfly fact

Crab spiders are the same colour as certain flowers, making them difficult to spot when they hide inside. The spiders leap out and catch butterflies when they land.

This flower mantid has caught a butterfly.

22

This wren is feeding a caterpillar to its chick.

Eaten by birds

Caterpillars are a favourite food of many birds, especially when the birds are raising chicks. A pair of parent birds may catch one caterpillar every minute to feed their young. Caterpillars are also eaten by other animals, such as hedgehogs, larger insects and spiders.

As so many caterpillars are eaten, butterflies lay lots of eggs so that some survive to become adults.

Butterfly camouflage

Butterflies have many ways of avoiding being eaten. One way is to blend in with the background so that they are difficult to spot. This is called **camouflage**. For example, the comma butterfly has wings with a ragged edge. This shape helps it to blend in with plants such as brambles. Glasswing butterflies have clear patches on their wings so that they are more difficult to see.

The green colouring of this caterpillar helps it to blend in with the colours of the plant stem.

24

The wings of this dead-leaf butterfly are shaped and coloured to look like dead leaves.

Caterpillar disguises

Caterpillars cannot move very quickly so they rely on camouflage to stay hidden. Many caterpillars are green, so that they cannot be seen among the leaves.

Some caterpillars are coloured and shaped so that they look like a twig. When they are still, they are almost impossible to spot.

Butterfly

The caterpillars of the orchard swallowtail butterfly are camouflaged to look like bird droppings.

fact

Warning colours

Some butterflies and caterpillars are poisonous and this protects them from **predators**. They have brightly coloured wings to warn hunters that they are not good to eat. The main warning colours used are usually red, yellow and black.

The yellow, orange and black wings of the monarch butterfly are a warning that it is poisonous.

Copy cats

Some butterflies copy the colours of poisonous butterflies even though they are not poisonous themselves. This is called mimicry. Predators think the mimics are bad to eat and leave them alone.

The caterpillar of the owl butterfly has a scary head to frighten away predators.

False heads

Some caterpillars have other ways of putting off predators. Some have false heads at the end of their abdomen to distract the predator and to protect their head from attack. Others have hairs that irritate the predator's mouth.

Butterfly

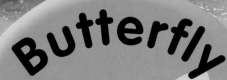

The monarch butterfly gets its poison from milkweed, the plant that its caterpillar eats.

fact

Butterflies under threat

Butterflies around the world are in danger and some species have already become **extinct**. The main reason for this is that people are destroying the butterflies' habitats, such as rainforests and grasslands.

Another problem is that many brightly coloured butterflies are caught and killed to sell as tourist souvenirs.

These bright butterflies were caught in the forests of South America. They have been killed and pinned inside display cases.

Conserving butterflies

Butterflies can be saved by protecting their habitat. Farms can also be set up to breed butterflies so they do not have to be caught in the wild. Sometimes it is possible to reintroduce butterflies to places where they have died out.

Butterfly farmers do not collect caterpillars from the wild. They rear the butterflies to sell to collectors.

Butterfly

Villagers in Papua New Guinea are rearing rare birdwing butterflies to sell in order to pay for new schools and hospitals.

fact

Life cycle

The female butterfly lays eggs. Usually a caterpillar hatches from each egg in less than ten days. The caterpillar moults about five times to reach full size. Then it turns into a pupa. Inside the pupa, the body of the caterpillar is rearranged into an adult butterfly. When fully formed, the adult butterfly pushes out of the pupa and flies away.

Butterfly eggs

Caterpillar

Pupa

Emerging adult butterfly

Glossary

abdomen third part of an insect's body behind the thorax

antenna (plural **antennae**) feelers used by butterflies to detect smells and to balance

camouflage the way the colours or shape of an animal's body blends in with the background, making it more difficult to spot the animal

caterpillar the worm-like, growing stage in the life cycle of a butterfly

compound eyes large eyes made up of many parts

Equator an imaginary line round the centre of the Earth

extinct when there are no more left alive

insect an animal with three body parts – head, thorax and abdomen – with three pairs of legs and usually two pairs of wings

mate to breed

metamorphosis a change in shape or appearance, for example, when a caterpillar changes into a butterfly

migrate a regular journey from one part of the world to another

moult to shed skin

nectar the sugary liquid produced by many flowers

predator an animal that hunts and kills other animals

proboscis the feeding tube of certain insects

proleg the leg-like stumps on a caterpillar's abdomen

pupa (plural **pupae**) structure in which the body of the caterpillar is rearranged into an adult butterfly

thorax the second part of the body of an insect

Index